These new poems are to do with frontiers and the interaction of different worlds. One section discusses our relationship with the past, another explores urban consciousness; a third group is set along the archetypal boundary of the seashore; other poems hover at the border between outer and inner worlds.

Tony Lucas lives and works in London. He has recently been reading for a MA in Medieval History, and is now fronting a major restoration project for the church of St George the Martyr, Southwark, where he is Rector. He has been Corresponding Editor for an American magazine for several years, and has promoted a series of readings in St George's Crypt, in association with *Ambit* magazine. He is married with two sons. Stride published his previous collection *Too Far For Talk*; the author is also one of three writers included in *Private Cities*.

Rufus At Ocean Beach

– *Stride* –

Other Stride books by the same author:

Too Far For Talk

Private Cities
(with Joel Lane & Robin Lindsay Wilson)

A Poem For Buddy
(contributor)

Earth Ascending
(contributor)

RUFUS AT OCEAN BEACH

Tony Lucas

RUFUS AT OCEAN BEACH
First edition 1999
© Tony Lucas
All rights reserved

ISBN 1900152 36 3

Cover design by Neil Annat

Acknowledgements
A Package Of Poems (Nexus), *A Touch Of Flame* (Lion),
Acumen, Ambit, Christian, The Formalist (USA), *The Lyric* (USA),
National Poetry Competition Anthology (The Poetry Society),
Omnibus, Orbis, Ore, Outposts, Poems On The Buses,
Poetry Life, Seven South Coast Poets (Lyceum Press),
South Bank University Competition Anthology (South Bank University),
Smiths Knoll, South Coast Poetry Journal, Vision On (Ver Poets).

Published by
Stride Publications
11 Sylvan Road, Exeter
Devon EX4 6EW

CONTENTS

Evidences

Insecurities

Shorelines

Making Space

Evidences

THE ARCHAEOLOGIST

I have made her out of shards,
from splintered yellow bone, one
rusted knife blade and the siftings
of a midden. Now I could tell you
what she ate, her general health
and social standing. We can approach
a date, guess who her rulers were
and map their routes of trade.

She has no face, no manners, and
no means of speaking for herself;
yet she can stand against the landscape,
act as an extra, dressing
the middle distances of history.

Among the broken pots, the walnut shells,
fragments of tell-tale patterning,
it is as if I fashioned her
with my own hands, feeling, almost
the grey mud filling out between
my fingers as her contours formed.

Now by my careful science
I have fathered her, so I desire
that she be fruitful in the evidence
she bears, and will embrace
this bonding of her name with mine,
as wax that takes the imprint
of the mind, compliant,
matrix of our shared posterity.

A PAPYRUS IN THE ASHMOLEAN

Time plays strange tricks:
      'A scribe writes home
      to tell two ladies of the family
      he is well
      and that they shouldn't worry over him.
      He, on the other hand
      is worried about them.
      Let them pray for his safe return.'

A civil servant's message home –
the heartfelt commonplaces saved
from the wreck of thirty centuries,
while an untold wealth of poems,
paintings, annals rot away.

Split and discoloured, behind glass,
the brash black letters, briskly dashed
across their sheet, can short-circuit
all those years touching us
closer than the bas-reliefs, the amulets,
canopic jars that cluster dustily around –
with common values, proof against decay.

THE LAST DEFENDERS

Centuries afterward
when we uncovered them
sprawled in a dug-out
they looked almost relaxed,
legs draped across each other,
heads laid back. Wasted,
of course, stripped to the bare bone,
one with his skull smashed –
unless it just collapsed with time.

They had that empty smile,
mocking, sardonic, as if to say
'Well, what else did you expect?
– the bloody standard?
swords that we fell on?
grey corpses hacked in two?

We waited in our hole because
we knew of nothing else to do,
nowhere to go. We kept on hoping
for the best. And when the worst
caught up with us, we greeted it
as something closer to relief.
It was all over in a day.
After a thousand years you don't
remember pain. Save up your pity.
You could live through
another version of the same.'

IN SEARCH OF ST NINIAN

Down at the landing place, damp winds
blow off the Irish Sea, raking
the grey ramp cut in the shoulder
of a stoney promontory:
a place the map says you should see,
but little here detains you.

Smart skirted tourist guides
now occupy the Priory and
its precincts. Archaeologists
have filletted the legend
with their illustrative maps,
decoded post-holes, artefacts –
making the solitary man of faith
drop out of sight, engulfed
in scholarly equivocation
and bright merchandise.

For the determined, it is said
he also had a place of refuge
even from his own community,
some three miles down the coast.
Sparse signposts to a muddy track
that winds through half a mile of woodland,
ending on rain-washed cobbles
of an isolated beach.
The oystercatcher starts up, piping
its warning, beats across the waves.

No one could prove he ever used
this cave, set at the far end
of the bay, over the cobbled shelves
of grincing stones; but, down the years,
pilgrims have followed in his name,
under the moisture that drops down

the cliff, curtaining an entrance
grand as some cathedral arch.
No deep recesses, only sheltered space
floored with clean shingle, framed
with a view along the headlands.

Nobody comes all afternoon.
Chambered stone seems eloquent
of presence worth the journey
of a pilgrim or a saint. A place
of worship in the changing light,
to let the rhythm of the sea's swell
wash away whatever cares
of a community, the childishness
of elders, passions of mediocrity.

A space to read the text of quartz veins
scribbled through the stones,
to learn the lesson of the sea pink,
the icon of a fulmar's flight.

Whithorn, Galloway

THE RAID

Our bird-prow breasted ocean bite
eight days and nights.
We made new landfall
at a grassy island
lying some half-league off
a coast of broad white sand.

There found a stone burgh
tended for some absent lord
by silent, black-smocked men.
They ran before our first attack,
no weapon coming to their hands.
We cut them down in fields,
on sand, and even cowering
on their knees within the darkness
of the great stone barn.

A few had put to sea
in small boats, but we let them go;
all they took with them
was a wooden box of bones
– or so the captives swore.
This was poor sport –
and not one woman found
in any corner of the island.

Even their treasure hoard was meagre
– one gold cup, a little coin,
the rest just skin and parchment,
sheets and bundles everywhere
scratched over with the never-ending
black runes of their scribe.

What sheep our boats would carry
we drove off, then fired
the buildings, drank their wine,
consoled each other
this had been the easiest
day's work we'd ever known.

Yet always afterward
a feeling haunts me
that we rowed for home
leaving behind us, unaware,
some greater wealth they owned.

RUFUS AT OCEAN BEACH

The king is on his boogie board,
bragging and cursing in the breakers
like some red-head bull seal. He is
attended by the usual crew
of promising young men – oiled bodies
worked up in the gym, sport
in the daytime, drunk at night.

The queen does not come to the beach.
She is concerned for her complexion.
Other ladies from the court
spread towels and wax their legs, attended
by those gentlemen his majesty's
good pleasure is unlikely to require
today. Bikini straps may sometimes
be unloosed, they say. The king
thinks little of such laxity.

My lord the Bishop sits among
the dunes, his entourage around.
A chaplain reads the morning office
while his lordship gazes silently
to sea. Maybe he is reflecting
on some mystery, or thinks
of the archbishop and his journey
into exile. Most probably
he reckons that the king will be
expecting him to pay for lunch.

I see that Eadric's Seafood Shack
is offering pan-fried lampreys with
a garlic mayonnaise – tossed
on a bed of rocket and roast peppers
– as their special for today.
His majesty could go for that.

Ranulf the Chancellor is busy
with his laptop, under the shadow
of the only clump of trees. He will
wait patiently until the king
is in a mood to sign state papers,
then dispatch his minions
to serve a writ, collect a fee.

People complain about the taxes;
but the king will be commissioning
a new design of longbow, and
he will not take the field without
support of Flemish mercenaries.

The papers carry rumours that
King Louis moves against the Vexin;
will the Court of Anjou stay his hand?
More news of trouble in Jerusalem.
Another anti-Pope declared.
The price of worsted still holds firm.

The king calls for a bigger board,
gets up to ride and, for a moment,
looks invincible, astride
the surge of power beneath his feet:
then he is down and floundering
in the surf, quite suddenly at risk
as all the young bloods move to his
assistance – Walter Tirel riding
like an arrow through the spray.

CASTLING

The Ministry now mows the lawn
and weeds the tidy gravel path,
fences off crumbling towers and marks
each century's building on a chart.

Such an approach to history
is rational and not to be deplored;
but also safe and rather dull.
The school kids come here and are bored.

And after all, such care won't stop
the algae eating through the stone,
nor re-make broken pediments
and corbels time has overthrown.

Others now treasure ruins for
the harebell that grows in the wall,
conserve the fairy foxglove where
it thrives inside the Greater Hall.

Although they fence off battlements
that drop abruptly into air,
they can't stop fancies taking off
while climbing up some crooked stair,

along bent passageways that lead
to draughty jakes or arrow slits,
imagining blood and tortured limbs
dropped down the deep unlighted pits;

squinting up hollow-towered dark
or down a dank, slime-coated well,
to feel the echo of a breath
that travelled from some rim of hell.

Sloppy, perhaps, to view the past
in terms of lurid sentiment;
yet sometimes there's more life in what
sensation-seeking minds invent.

DOWN TO EARTH

Inside the abbey ruins
two stone bishops, carved
in eucharistic vestments
giving their benediction,

have been taken down
for safety from some high niche;
now, in their corner, propped
at a tipsy angle, they become

two shaggy bearded men
in funny hats, long mouldering garments
to keep out the cold,
loitering beneath the arches

holding out broken hands
to beg, and muttering
the derelict's gruff salutation
of 'Gor bless yer, guv'.

AMATEUR

He always knew his kitchen plot
lay in the oldest part of town,
and, turning up a decorated shard,
decided to forget the celery bed
and just keep digging down.

Amongst assorted earthenware
he found a bent fork, clay pipe stem,
small mechanism crusted up
with rust. He almost missed the sliver
of a coin, clipped round the edges
and too rubbed for him to read.
A scratch revealed its silvery sheen.

So, after that he went more carefully,
stood to his waist now in the trench
he'd dug. Then he began uncovering
bones – old ones, and yellowed,
some of them cracked. Although he had
no real way to know, their size
suggested they were human.

Was this the corner of some graveyard?
plague pit? or the evidence
of long-forgotten crime? History
began to darken. Once, he had thought
about the past as friendly, full
of the faces of lost ancestors,
waiting to welcome him, display
their curious ways. Now he began
to smell brutality and fear, lives
lived in desperate ignorance,
lost reservoirs of pestilence,
still able to corrupt the present day.

His dreams began to trouble him.
He was not sorry to be interrupted
by the rain; and, when a corner
of his ill-made trench collapsed,
he took the hint and shovelled back
the spoil heap, burying all evidence,
tamping it down, spreading this blanket
on the years, then bedding in
the crisp, fresh vegetables between.

Insecurities

THE POET COUGHING

The tissue of his lungs became so delicate
it seemed the insubstantial air did violence
to tender membrane. Each breath would catch
with grating scratchiness through frail
capillaries. The microscopic poisons
sucked in would coagulate in sticky
residues, lodging beneath his heart.
He tried to cough up gently, ease out offending
matter, but the process of dislodgement,
once begun, had to continue till
he fetched out every irritating speck.

Those little flowers of blood flecked on
white handkerchiefs did not dismay him.
They were just tokens of a bloom within.
There was a satisfaction in that moment
when you seemed to reach down, right
into the bottom, scoop up the last grey morsel
of the clotted phlegm. It took so much
out of him. Clearing a lung could leave him
prostrate half the afternoon. Brief peace
ensued, as he dropped back against
the pillow, though he knew that soon
the cycle would start up again.

How long this weakness had been incubating
was impossible to say. For years
he had been dying of the malady.
Living so long with his affliction,
he could not imagine being free.
If some strange doctor were to come and cure him,
what sort of life could he then lead?
Without the focus of this aggravating
chemistry, what would his purpose be?

ALMS

Sitting in the foyer, drinking coffeee,
I could see the clarinettist where
he hunched to leeward of a statue's plinth,
faint strains of 'Stardust' filtering from chill air,

and saw the tall guy in an open raincoat,
colour of buttermilk, passing with that
slight swift stoop to flick a weighted coin
so neatly in the woodwind's upturned hat –

able, at once, to look magnaminous
and casual. You either have that art of slipping
in and out of easy condescension,
or have not. Same quandary as with tipping.

Rather than deal with the embarrassment
of fumbling some inappropriate amount
into a palm much more discreet, to lug
two heavy bags all down the stairs will count,

for some of us, an easier way of getting
to the taxi rank. Yet that's erroneous:
every cabbie springs another trap,
making us feel ripped off, or parsimonious.

Practice may help, or having enough to spare
that you don't worry about margins. That's not
the reason even buying *The Big Issue*
feels a challenge to avoid: it's what

the whole transaction tells of status, class,
and any sort of guilt it may flush out
for seeming better off. Also about exposure,
how the self-conscious put themselves about.

Does giving money leave you feeling worse
or better? It will surely come across
in how it's done. Easier to look stylish
if you basically don't give a toss.

ONE THAT GOT AWAY

I was just changing to go out
at half past six, a warm June evening,
choosing a white shirt, canvas shoes
and gazing through the window
when I saw this policeman
clambering across the garden fence.
So, leaning out, I asked
'What's going on?', thinking I ought to know,
and he stopped in the middle of the new-mown lawn
and said 'We think
there's something hiding in your garden.'

Then he picked his way
round the tomatoes,
searching behind the raspberry canes,
and came back carrying a bright red helmet.
'Didn't you hear the crash?' he asked,
and I said 'No'.
Three Rovers and a Transit, by this time,
had almost blocked the street
and there were policemen climbing
on the garden walls as far as you could see.

We all went out,
feeling it was the right thing to look interested,
and joined the neighbours making sure
it wasn't our car that got hit.
But it turned out to be a stolen motorbike
some guy had ditched, but no one
seemed to see which way he ran,

and it was very warm, people were thinking
about going out and meeting friends for drinks,
or getting ready for their holidays
while, one by one, the policemen all went on
to other things, taking the bike as evidence,
and we went back inside.

Just as I finished dressing,
I looked out and saw
the red crash helmet had been left behind,
plumb in the middle of our neat green lawn,
a circus nose, bright
and abandoned, unidentified.

MISADVENTURE

Somebody found him in the stairwell
of a block of flats – no sign of violence,
with money in his pockets,
dressed in presentable clean clothes.

The parents wait beside
the telephone he never used.
They have retained
soft accents of the countryside.

Their home has the provisional feeling
of a cheap hotel, as if
the furnishings all came by chance.
They do not seem to have his photograph.

The city, thirteen floors below,
– a jewel box spilled,
spangling exhausted highways,
mapping the energies of night.

The lights spell out a landscape
they have never learned to read.
Somewhere down there they lost him,
in the dark interstices.

Death seems like another
bureaucrat; habit suggests
he is best spoken to politely.
They are not expected to complain.

This is a chapter of a story
told too often down
the centuries. What seems important
is that they should maintain

a certain dignity – something that feels
worthy of past hopes, of future
aspirations – no matter now
if these were inappropriate to him.

A VACANT LOT

Sheds or garages knocked down, nothing
that anyone has missed, leaving a small site
too nondescript to call an eyesore: patches
of concrete, half a wall, dumped bedding
where the corrugated fence got breached.

Only the kids find use for this lost space,
gathering in its quiet corners to conspire;
or one lone child may fill an empty hour
batting a ball against the brickwork,
idly elaborating on some useless skill.

In every crevice grass or flowers have grown,
an elder rooted in the corner; on the wall
tough clumps of ragwort cling and bloom,
and year by year the willowherb grows tall,
launching its feathered seeds across the town.

THERE'S NO PLACE...

Soon after six, in fading light
and coming off the motorway,
he found himself following a car
much like his own – metallic grey,

a one-point-five saloon – travelling
up the slip road, left toward town.
He tried to overtake; the driver
seemed to keep his sped around

the same, and there was heavy traffic,
people going home. He waited
till they reached the outskirts, but
the other car anticipated

his fork westwards, where they queued
past all the shops. To his surprise,
it took the short cut, round behind
the hospital. To scrutinize

the stranger he moved up behind,
jumping the lights to follow close,
over the staggered junction, through
the estate – until it felt almost

as if predicted, when the car
turned up his street and signalled right,
just over halfway down. Now spellbound
by the hypnotic winking light,

he watched the vehicle swing across
to occupy the parking space
of his three-bedroomed house. The road
was full, as usual, no place

he could pull in. He drew up short
for long enough to see a man
about his own age getting out,
walking across with key in hand

opening his own front door. He thought
he glimpsed his wife in welcome, there
in the shadowed hall... A car horn barked
behind, moving him round the square

of streets. When he came back again
the house looked distanced, self-possessed,
shut up against him. Would his arrival
be some kind of palimpsest?

There had to be an explanation.
He always came home this time of day.
Or was he trammelled in confusion?
Must he now park two streets away,

walk home, confront the mystery?
Go in and find, perhaps, a thin-lipped
in-law on the beige settee?
Confusion of his wife unzipped

for some dark stranger, with the kids
next door to watch TV? The eager
salesman for insurance, God forbid,
or double-glazing, to beleaguer

his arrival? Might it be simpler
to accept he'd got the whole thing wrong,
lived someone else's life, or dreamed
about a place he could belong?

Then he could just drive on, a chapter
ended; drive through the dark and rain,
embrace whatever dawn might bring,
and never go back home again.

WHAT GETS LOST

Veined marble, two carnations,
and a white bone china teapot:

the four o'clock light sliced
through venetian blinds
sections the table top,

stippling a summer frock
and falls across the page
of poetry, angled
in contrapuntal stripes,

cross-hatching, as if it meant
to cancel out the lines.

TRUCE

The fox's footprints circle round
the outer margins of the lawn,
   melting through snow to grass.

Devoid of incident, the world
stays smothered, locked under cover, while
   the new year starts to pass.

A Christmas tree, half-buried, lies
where they pushed it through the doorway,
   like a cat, or erring child;

but seasonal quarrels have now ebbed;
those who the snow shuts in together
   seem more reconciled

to the continuation of domestic
life. The cold cuts deep enough
   to paralyse the will.

No one will idly twist a knife,
rub salt, or ruffle fur, endurance
   is the present skill.

The winter sunlight fades. Briefly
the silent garden is disrupted
   by a shouting bird;

but he is just scaremongering;
grey snow and stillness coalesce
   to make him seem absurd.

NEXT DAY AT THE CLUB

Ash of a generation's smoking,
powdered in every mottled inch
of maculated carpet, makes
morning-after senses flinch;

it mingles with the sticky drinks,
sweet spillage souring overnight
on every ersatz surface lining
this padded cave. Blinking from daylight,

eyes distinguish sombre reds,
dejected greens and tarnished chrome.
Back in the gloom, a tired woman
talks into the telephone.

The barman is restocking shelves,
busy behind his shuttered grille,
polishing glasses – mundane work
amid such louche environs; still,

someone must balance up the books
and fix the licence, hire bands,
rig up the set each night, and hope
some bubble of delight expands.

Shorelines

SUMMER, 1945

A small boy on the beach
that stretches to the sky.
No one else in sight. He is
studying the scratches
marked out by his spade, absorbed
in learning the way water
fills up holes in sand.

Only the camera watches him.
It is the earliest holiday
he will remember, first taste
of seaside – paddling in shallows,
treading corrugated sand
to prod the stranded jellyfish,
discover curled pink shells.

Streaked slabs of concrete line
the shore. There is a war
still finishing somewhere, and he has yet
to meet his father. During the months
ahead, there will be soldiers
coming home, school with hard
playgrounds, babies being born.

This is not a place they'll come
on holiday again. Yet
he'll retain a sense of safety
in the emptiness, a clearing sky,
before the coming of what
they called 'peace', but which
meant something else for him.

FIRST LIGHT

The plover, squat upon the morning rocks,
tucks in his bib and runs to breakfast.
On sheets of glass along the water's edge
a parliament of gulls debates the passage
of two fishing boats that drift the long horizon.
The sun mounts through citrine to white,
melting a fat moon on the skillet of the sky.

We have not deserved this clarity of light,
the rinsing air, the waters rippling and benign.
This morning is a gift, and asks for no return.
Men with their dogs stand gazing out to sea
at nothing, simply for pleasure of pure sight.
And soon we cannot look into the risen sun,
but turn about to watch the way it paints
bright shades of welcome on the waking town.

DOGFISH DECONSTRUCTION

'I expect you've written a poem
about the fish', she said to him
when he came back along the beach,
following a slick and smelly rim

of jetsam, washed up on the shingle,
crab-shell or carrion every couple of feet,
discarded from two-dozen drifters,
battered quorum of the local fleet.

In fact, he hadn't. So predictable
a subject didn't seem worth contemplation:
yet, he'd be hard put to deny
the awareness of a certain fascination

with the dogfish, fledgling sharks,
their cold, glazed eyes and freckled skin,
some with their guts pulled out
by seagulls, others more akin

to plastic toys that eight-year olds
might relish, plucked from a wholesome range
of monsters for the family bath.
At least dead fish would make a change

from carcasses of moorland sheep.
But why should they exercise attraction?
Was this some spasm of the nuclear angst?
Just middle-aged morbidity? or a reaction

against soft suburban dreams?
Memento mori, after all, was one
of the enduring themes of verse.
Was it because a generation

who have never been to war – and, spared
the ravages of famine or the plague,
have rarely even had to nurse Aunt Ethel
to her messy end – become so vague

and squeamish about facts no longer talked of
over teacups, or made jokes on at the bar,
so need to turn to Nature, much as
our forebears once had similar

resort to birds and bees when sex
had such unmentionability?
Maybe these subjects are the backsides
of a spoiled gentility.

But who seriously complains?
Thank God it's not a place in which
you're likely to find human bodies
gutted and stinking in a roadside ditch.

Hearing the News, he thought, perhaps
it's better to be thankful, and not wish
for worse than we've already got.
Better to write a poem on dead fish.

SWIFTS AT HODBARROW

remembering Norman Nicholson

I cannot read this jumbled site –
its pitted roadways leading nowhere,
thickets and sea wall heaped of spoil,
Over a lifetime you had spelled out
every phase – of industry and its decline,
the loss of livelihoods, nature indomitable
in a rare wildflower, all that dismantlement,
the levelling and flood. It is a scraped
and plundered manuscript, now overwritten
with accounts unbalanced, history revised.

I did not come looking for bee-orchid
or the bloody cranesbill, only to watch
the grebes and shelduck on a salt lagoon.
But more and more I'm looking upward
into evening air, a whirl of blades,
soundlessly sabring, slicing around us
as if juggled by some phantom thrower
of dark knives; their stubby beaks
shovelling at unseen prey, swifts soar above
your scrubby tips and waste-heaped shore.

They have no footing in our element.
The bird book names their habitat 'the sky';
wild wheeling fantasies, elusive as
the images we long to capture – almost
to hand, then swirling far beyond
our earthbound grasp, where only
in the mind we seem to follow.
Death is the place they come to land.

AT THIS MOMENT IN TIME...

Karen and Dave come to the beach,
catching a couple of hours' blue sky
on Sunday afternoon; though each
is slightly overweight, they lie

at ease. He sleeps off drinks at lunch,
three fingers slipped inside the belt
of her black trousers. She has bunched
her tee-shirt to expose a welt

of pallid midriff, kicked off her shoes
and placed them on the unread paper
to prevent the breeze unfurling news
of shootings on the Irish border,

courtroom accounts of sex and lies,
adverts to sell the newest pension plan
– oblivious to the background cries
of children play-fighting in the sand.

Above their heads, a crumbling syncline
of the Devonian shale gives hold
to sea-pinks; wheeling in, where sunshine
catches that millenial fold,

a seagull perches. To its yearning call
worries of job, of health or mortgage,
melt in the sun and life seems all
about the level of the sports page.

A small plane trails across the bay
bright streamers for the amusement park.
She shuts long lashes on the common day
to watch her blood cells dancing, dark.

MAN WITH DOG

The summer afternoon turns fractious.
Down by the sea's edge, where the children dig
and grandmas paddle in bright flowery frocks,
a man stands with a small dog in his arms:

a short man, well into middle-age,
with blue striped shirt and flapping trousers;
one you might picture more at ease
carrying a bag of work-worn tools.
The dog is delicate and curly-haired,
a kind it would be no surprise to see
with bows of pale-blue ribbons on its head.

They look incongruous, beside the surly ocean
– yet, in the manner that he holds his charge,
something is oddly touching –
as though the sea had frightened it,
or that he feared it might jump in and drown;
as if he had himself some talent,
which the rest of life had under-used,
for shielding high-strung, fragile lives
from all the world's rough elements can do.

STILL LIFE

I pick a cobble off the beach:
it has the temperature of flesh,
touch of a generous warmth
stored from the day's bright sun.

To handle these round contours,
finger the texture of its mottled skin,
judge the poised weight, is almost
to believe you hold a living thing,

and that some flinty heart is beating
deep within. If it were thrown,
or dropped and broken, you might
even get blood from a stone.

A SALT LAGOON

Even the gulls do little to disturb the quietness,
just stand about in shallow water
stretching the occasional wing.
A heron languidly comes drifting in.
Two cormorants have sat all afternoon upon a board.

The water doesn't seem to flow,
nor any ripples break along the level shore;
no other motion than the pattern winds make
moving across the surface into reeds
that whisper round a corner of the creek.

It is as if I'd travelled all the week to reach
this point. People have called these muddy inlets
'desolate'. No doubt it is enhanced
by lingering sunlight, and a late October breeze
that even now lacks any cutting edge.

Yet, after helicopters clatter overhead,
and even after winter storms, calm such as this
returns, and nothing seems to change along the shore.
It's like a place that's always waiting for us,
deep in stillness, asking – Do you look for more?

THE DROWNED CITY

Earlier years have seen whole houses drop
down the cliffside; streets, quays and churches,
monasteries and shops, fall from the town
that once ruled all this coast. And when the graveyards
came away, the tombs were broken open, rude bones
strewn on beaches or left jutting from the clay.

The sea now bides its time, is almost deferential
as it breaks along these beaches, quietly digests
the ancient grist of swallowed streets and churches,
skulls of the paupers and of burgesses, flushed
from their final resting place by each past storm.
Only the martins dare to make a home up there today.

The sea shows nothing; patches of sunlight chase
across the grey. Nothing to suggest the acreage
of ruins strewn across its bed. It keeps close secrets.
Divers have groped down into the cold and dark,
fumbled through wreckage, guessed at a site or two,
and brought back uncommunicative stones.

The ghosts do not much haunt this quiet coast,
even the memories now seem lost beneath the sea.
Sailors no longer hear the drowned bells toll.
There just remains a dream of ordered streets
and open houses, garlands of wafted weed, fish gliding
in and out of windows, and a parish kept for every shoal.

Making Space

GETTING AWAY

At last we're off the motorway
and slowing to a view of hills,
glint of an estuary unravelling
to the south. And this is what
we left the city to discover –
the verges white with hawthorn, cows
in the fields, small furry creatures
squashed along the carriageway –
announcements of the countryside.

Now we can look out for nature trails,
for picnic sites; get out the books
on birds and flowers; pull on the boots,
the windproof clothes; plan a good walk
to some place with a pub for lunch;
let loose the dog; find out which gardens
serve the best cream tea. Tomorrow
we can all relax – sleep late,
go somewhere with some decent shops.

AWAY FROM IT ALL...

The silence of the place embraced us,
on arrival, like a gracious host,
easing the irritance of travel,

laying us down to dreamless sleep.
It seemed a kind of miracle
to sit and watch the sun go down

beyond the supper table, swallows
give way to bats, and never a car,
a plane, to interrupt that calm.

After a few first restful days though,
silence becomes insistent company,
crowding in closer night by night,

till I grow wary of it. Lying
awake now, in the deepest hours,
I hear each tiny sound it brings –

a settling timber, birds in the vineyard,
the watchdog on an adjacent hill –
each magnified, and by imagining

conspiracies, startling myself,
transform this gentle friend into
our enemy. For too long we have learned

to fear such quiet, cannot conceive
of silence being other than a prelude
to the monster crashing through the screen.

My sleep dissolves in acids
of an anxious vigil, wide-eyed until
– as if to mock me for foregoing

trustful dream – slowly, a pale dawn
seeps between the shutters to illuminate
our long, unwavering peace.

À LA MUSÉE DE L'ART MODERNE

Angular white spaces, acres
of pale wood floor, window shafts
that frame the unexpected view
of fountains, or assemblages
of iron plate, glimpses of roadway
where smart trams go gliding by:
cool modernism, keeping out
the sun's glare, sticky midday heat.

The broad abstractions on the walls
say nothing – lending only colour,
texture, to the white geometry.
To inhabit such clear space
would make life simple, you might think.

They do not see it that way –
the curators, the administrators,
delegates attending this week's
colloquy on deeper meanings...
sémiotique... spacialité...
Speeches in the conference room
drift on, in muted lighting, heavy
with terms. Words of translators
frequently evade translation.

The sluices of the dam are open
wide today. The river surges,
high in its embankment, ferrying
debris from the passes, folds
through tight arches of the bridge, chaffing
and burnishing their marble feet.

One in each hand, a file of mothers
lead away their infants, from
the playground in the park. Most
carry knapsacks full of juice
and wipes, slowly, heads bowed
processing to the traffic of the town.

It feels inviting just to linger
here, in dedicated space, taking
your ease in this black leather,
chrome-framed chair, placed
for aesthetics rather than convenience
– yet you suspect the restless camera
will be wondering why you sit
so long, someone start asking
what it is you're writing down?

It would be more acceptable
behaviour to get up and pace
the polished floor, pausing
to rub the chin, ponder, perhaps,
on matters of perception, *actualité*,
but circulating always with the flow,
toward the coffee bar, the eventual
exit back onto the noisy street – *recréé*
cependant, having viewed the show.

CHANGE OF USE

Housemartins, thistledown, light aeroplanes,
criss-cross a sky of faultless blue.
Red cottage roofs doze in the hedgerows,
while a breeze sways ripening seed-heads
far across the fields of yellow light.

No one has sowed these fields or grazed
the paddocks all this year. The barn
collapses on its knees, shipwrecked
in burgeoning elder and the nettles' swell.

They own more pleasure boats than tractors
in this village now. Plans are in hand
for the conversion of the manor
to a luxury hotel – replacing
jobs, paying to keep the tiles in shape.

Observe the solitary heron
gliding down the brook, oxeyes
and hawkbit blooming in the fallow,
dry rustle of the hogweed heads.

Soon they will drive a golf-course clear
across these meadows, bulldoze the pasture,
reconstituting an entire landscape –
hillocks and sandpits, little lakes,
that manicured perfection of flagged greens.

OUT OF TOWN

Native of the city, bred
to central heating, the hermetic
double-glazing of his fourth floor flat,

he has forgotten how the wind
howls down a chimney, rattles old windows
and insinuates each chink and gap.

The cottage holds no fear
of burglars, street fights
or political unrest;

merely the secret infiltration
of the damp through ancient walls,
insects invading every crack;

all that lush foliage, dabbing at windows,
patient through centuries,
waiting for its moment to attack.

PRACTISING SOLITUDE

I

Somewhere, a shutter
has worked loose, bangs
on a wall, echoes
all through the house.

Harping at nerve ends,
wind from the south
has set the guard dog
barking for no reason.

Each day the poplar chatters
after sunset; but tonight
all kinds of trees raise voices
in a chorus of unease.

Tonight no bats came,
clinically to knife
among the leaves, as in
propitiation of the dark.

Bodies lie doubled
round the sour knot
of old anxieties, we hoped
had been left far behind

in cities of the north,
but curdle in the bowel now
– an aftertaste of fear, or
far too much cheap wine.

Deep in the night
the wind shifts round,
a silence falls, and then
the clatter of a storm.

As thunder breaks,
we can relax, at length,
wrapped in its tumult,
we can sleep safe, at ease.

II

It's said that there were nuns here once,
though no one really seems to know.
Only a little chapel now survives,
set at the ridge's end, a snapped-off hull,
beached above vineyards, olive groves below.

Short rows of ageing cypress offer soft footfall
and a moment's shade to my approach.
The brickwork cracks along old fault lines,
much of the mortar gone. Brambles spew out
from cavities and overrun the roof;
the doors not painted for a generation,
loosely lashed up with curtain wire.

A chink of daylight, slanting through inner darkness,
shows a scrolled pediment, the dusty floor.
Maybe a dozen sisters could have knelt
sheltering in marbled silence from the sun.

Lizards now own the place, chasing across
the sun-baked bricks; one an emblazon, splayed
on the blistered surface of the door,
enamelled emblem of its change of use.

They are not spirits of departed sisters,
nor the small demons who have ousted them.
However reminiscent of the figments
used by artists, filling waste places

round a saint – to tease him and torment
his life of prayer – these are just denizens,
reclaiming what has been their own.

Not numinous, nor haunted, more
a domestic wherewithal, a small
familiar perched on the shoulder of the hill –
the place is a repository of presences
long been and gone, and lingering only
as my idle speculation in the sun.

III
It would be easy though
to summon up unblemished faces,
windblown robes, processing
in the early light, easy
to envy their community,
their corporate and supportive peace.

In truth, it would be tarnished
by the usual irritants: bad cooking,
petty tyrannies, the way
another sister scratched her nose.

And all that space for searching prayer
would get encroached upon
by routine offices, a regime
of the drab necessities of life.

Even the sternest, most ascetical,
of hermits often draws a crowd –
admirers, correspondents, each
a devourer of the peace they seek.

Maybe the truest solitaries
always are the crazies in the desert,
polishing shotguns, waiting
for their apocalypse to come,
to terminate the nightmares
of a noonday sun.

FROM THE REALMS OF GLORY

If we should speak of angels, your mind now
might picture Burne-Jones windows, full of
lank hermaphrodites with dropping wings;
at best, fix on the gilded herald to some
quattrocento saint; at worst, a pert child
in a nightie, winsome on a Christmas card,
replete with rakish halo, wand and star.

Yet when Ezekiel, on the banks of Chebar,
saw the cherubim come in a whirlwind
from the north in flashing clouds of fire,
running on straight feet like thunder,
under the beating wings' torrential roar,
between their four-fold shapes and faces
burnished in the arc of light, they bore
so terrible a brightness that the prophet
needed seven days recovering from the sight.

Daniel fell down unconscious on the ground
before one girdled round in gold, with eyes
of lightning: at the sound of whose
earth-shaking voice companions fled
for fear of what they could not even see.
On Patmos, John was shown angelic wars,
the bloody harvest of this world reaped in,
for good or ill, and heard seraphic music
and triumphant roars rising with smoke from golden
bowls. Earth's time and purpose being done.

Small wonder we have little left to say
of angels – seeing such fearful majesty
fade into pallid shadows now. But is it true
they waned because our understanding grew
too great to leave them place? Or are there
territories of inner soul or outer space

our minds have safely sealed away, so
manageable facts, that reason can align,
may make out ordered maps, a world amenable
to our control, secure against the threat
of all unruly grace or glory that might
scatter certainties in disarray, suggesting
the ineffable could still remain in play?

GOD FOR BREAKFAST

'It really is a statement about how...
what a weak view of the christian life we all have...'

Country Boy Diner, in that plaza where the motels are,
third lot along. Waitress in a mini-skirt at seven a.m.

'You're a good communicator, you've done
your homework, you've put together your message...'

Short stack of pancakes, fresh fruit on the side.
'...It all comes out fiery. Seventy people get saved that night.'

'I recognise that I don't meet these standards...'
Cinnamon toast, maybe some egges? 'Let me ask you this:

Is there some dimension of your spiritual life that you are
disappointed in?' How do you like them? Over and easy.

'They're only two people in my life, my wife and daughter...'
Strawberry Duet: experience a European Legend.

'...all these words we're using synonymously
for God's work...' *This delicate pastry waffle*

*fresh baked in our kitchen until crispy
and golden tan...* '...and not because you're judging me...'

'And then again, the point is not that it's sinful
or anything...' *Just the way it was in Belgium*

during the Renaissance. '...only to do what it is
you really want to do.' 'Well, let me say this here –

I can give you the freedom to do that.'
Served with fresh strawberries, in season.

'Walt, I've got an assignment I'd like you to do.'
Is everything all right here? More coffee?

Santa Barbara

MAKING A SPACE

Leaving the house before she wakes,
he walks away from work, toward
the shore. A woman's cough, the drizzle
of a radio, drift from an open
condominium window and
he crosses on the highway, where
the seconds count down with each
passing car. A calm comes off
the ocean, reaching like absolution
to his feet, slopping the margins,
stirring a scum of weed, crab claw,
bent cans. A greyness, damply settled
on the water, folds in its breath.
Bird tracks and worm casts stay imprinted
on the sand. No one has been before him.

Above a hidden shoal, sharp terns
swarm in a circle, storming the surface
with a hail of beaks. The heavy
pelicans steer right among them.
Great grey umbrellas, they fall
in the ocean, seeming they must surely
break their wings, yet somehow snap
shut in the nick of time. They look
so vulnerable to him, recall
the awkward child one fears too tender
to plunge through the wheeling world.

The klaxon of a solitary
coasting boat breaks one hoarse blast.
Only an hour or two and all this
will be baffled by the shimmer
of blue heat scorching off oil-scarred
concrete. He turns back, passing
an old Korean fisherman

who keeps his vigil on the ground
marked out between two slender rods
embedded in the sand. He seems
an emblem of what stillness can
encompass, in a place where
silence is denied, the day's
demands close in on every hand.

EL CAMINO REAL

The day we drove down to Laguna,
we had just come off the beach
to get ice-cream – I opted for
a double scoop of green pistachio –
and, right outside the shop, were benches
on the sidewalk, where we sat
and balanced our top-heavy cones.

There by the corner, reading at
the people eating ice-cream, was
this unshaved, probably unwashed, guy
– some kind of ageing hippy – and
I thought at first that it must be
his own bad poems he was drearily
intoning. Listening, however,
it became apparent that it was,
in fact, the Sermon on the Mount
he was delivering to us through
a toneless nasal whine, flat
as the mid-West plains.

Then one of the good people there,
as if inspired by pious recitation,
started to hand round paper tissues
– and you, reaching to take one, dropped
your ice-cream – nearly a dollar's worth
of Butter Pecan, splat on the neat
brick pavement, where it sat
until the embarassed tissue man
returned and, with stiff covers
torn off his glossy magazine,
contrived to shovel up the mess.

Our reciter, undeterred, had flipped
right over to the Twentieth Psalm,
and was now telling us, '*Some put
their trust in chariots, and some
in horses...*', but the time was passing
and we had to get back on the Freeway,
ahead of the apocalyptic rush for home;
and so we left them to their various
good works, to make for where
the rented Mercury was parked,
back up the hill, a copy of
the Thomas Guide under the dashboard,
ready to help us find the way to go.

EL SANTUARIO DE CHIMAYO

Quickly, the tourist stoops
to press his fingers
on the dusty floor, tentative,
self-conscious, he looks
around him before rubbing
a little of the sandy dirt
on his rheumatic joint.

Entering the narrow rooms
of healing, he had felt
the hot intensity
of desperate hope grip him
like claustrophobia. He thought
that he had come into some
kind of pawn shop of devotion.

Green robed madonnas
with the lips of cupids;
the Holy Child, frocked
with pink nylon and provided
with new baby shoes
for walking through the night.

I would like to share
with each and every one of you
the beautiful miracle that happened
to me on the fifth of August…

Echoes of Esquipulas –
the black Christ. The atmosphere
of prayer is palpable. Crutches
hang all along the wall
to testify the efficacious
power of Chimayo's dust.

Water and Bread – so why not
Dust? God in the elemental things.
Nothing for those who would disdain
to bend and touch the dirt,
who would not take it
to themselves for healing.

...while I was making tortillas
the Sacred Heart of Jesus
appeared in one of my tortillas...

He did not understand the boundaries
of miracle and magic – the meaning
of a dark cross studded
with milagros, or this garish fervour
of the tinsel, artifical flowers
and Christmas decorations,
piled up as offerings before
the doll-like figures of the saints.

Are not the rivers of Damascus
better...? *I would like*
to invite you all to my home
to see it... Heat from a hundred
candles in the narrow space
seems to be stifling his breath.

A bus delivers pilgrim ladies
who process in from the car park
singing, as he goes out,
stuffing a dollar in the box
and hardly daring flex
his aching joint – out
to the shade of cottonwoods,
a glare of sunlight on adobe walls.

New Mexico

ETHNIC ARTS

The commodities in stock
at *ETHNIC ARTS* seem heavy
with religious connotation:

Yoruba divination trays,
voodoo fetishes from Haiti,
processional crosses out of Mexico.

The apparatus of the world's belief
offered for sale to those
who won't know what to do with it.

Is it for Art? Ethnology? or
new contortions of good taste?
Close contact with the spiritual

has endowed these objects with
a whiff of numinosity,
some non-specific hallowing.

Maybe they can become a kind
of lucky charm, or low-key icon;
substitute for household gods,

somehow keep watch, guard fires,
channel the luck, attract
unfocused superstition.

Perhaps it offers a new market
for the poor, supplying
a Peruvian healer's amulets,

or Indonesian prayer drums,
to those who find themselves without
a route back into worship, but

to acquire it – treasure or trash –
by that one universal means
that's always understood: Faith, sir?
Will you be paying charge or cash?

A SMALL WORLD

English-to-Japanese – the smiling couple
open their dictionary across bare knees,
search for the meaning of *Tomorrowland*.
Germans and Filipinos pass them by,
cameras in every other hand, tee-shirts
that emblazon *Minnesota Kings,*
Nebraska or *Hawaiian Sun.*

Wind off the desert, boosting up temperatures
towards a hundred, cannot divert the slick
machinery of play. Given a passport
to be children for a day, provided
with a thousand means to spend more money,
nothing will deflect the placid crowd
queuing for rides, surging from doorways
demanding of each other, 'Was that fun?'

Nothing to give offence – no alcohol,
no sex – unless you count the bronzed beach
bodies in bright scanty colours, nubile
among the crowd. Wholesome youngsters manage
to appear as if they could enjoy
a long shift sweeping cigarettes and cans.

At least the bricks are real, the wrought iron
isn't plastic. Not even darkness here
is sinister. People stay biddable,
benign, lining the phoney streets. Only
the silver heart shape of a helium
balloon breaks free, floating above the treetops,
drifting away from music, coloured lights,
and lost soon in the blue Pacific night.

Disneyland, California

HIGH ABOVE THE BAY

The wind chimes tinkle
in among the pelargoniums,
the agapanthus waiting
for its ration of piped water
to switch on. The sun moves
round the deck, and yachts
drift lazily towards Tiburon.

A rented car, a borrowed house,
this view to suit a smooth
proconsul or a fat tycoon;
we might more readily expect
a broken temple on the headland,
than the marbled precincts
of the shopping malls, set on each
sacred site between the hills.

These outmost limits of
the Western world tune to routines
of profit and convenience;
more people live in comfort round
this shore than in whole provinces
of Rome or Christendom.

Rimmed by apotheosis
of the suburb now, the bay
is tranquil, safe from storms,
and little news about the Old World
with its wars and torments
filters through to interfere.

We sip our drinks and lean back
basking in the beauty of the view,
our being here – complicit guests
of all it means – already
learning not to dwell
uneasily on gulfs beneath.

We do not care to look down
at the frail struts holding up
this house, high in the treetops,
nor at the people who could never
hope to share our view.

The seismic boundary stretching
in its restless sleep,
substantiates that ancient serpent
always lurking down below,
the flaw in every fair appearance
underscoring the tectonic faults
across each human heart.

As tourists, we can thrill
to sunlight on the waters,
gleaming towers above a plume
of cloud; and need not linger long
on forces that could send
the whole supporting structure
slithering down its hillside
smothering smart restaurants
and moorings far below.

Sausalito, California

BEDROCK

The wall is topped with inch-thick
slabs of local slate
a day-long sun has warmed.

I stretch my vulnerable back
on their firm bed, reading
a book of similar thickness.

If I should tap a knuckle
on the slate, it sounds
a musical, assuring note –

as speaking with a voice
that one could trust. By morning
every slab will have become

cold as a gravestone; though
if sounded out, the same
beguiling voice will speak,
with solid, satisfying tone.

PUT OFF THE SCENT

He loved that country – felt at ease there right away,
fell into patterns of their speech, drove with the traffic,
lazed on beaches, walked in the quiet hills,
happy with all the quirks that made life different.

First time he noticed it – this curious odour
– he was staying in a cheap motel, and afterward
returned to find his own apartment, shut up
three days, seemed fusty with the same dull savour.

A brownish sort of smell, woody perhaps, dried out
but with astringency, even slightly decomposing.
Soon, he was picking up the same scent in
his rented car, in corridors of offices,

in cinemas and bars. Whether it came
from dirt in corners, roaches behind the wall,
or no more than the disinfectant used
to dampen other rankness, he was never sure.

He even smelt it out of doors. What first
had seemed a passing nuance, gradually began
to dominate his sense, pervading each experience,
tainting his whole enjoyment of the place.

It grew into a presence he could not efface,
reminder he did not belong. Where he'd been happy
there as anywhere, it was this scent
that turned his stomach, leaving him sick for home.

TOO FAR FOR TALK

'These are carefully made poems... this calm voice from an uncalm place is an enjoyable one, full of feeling, clear-sighted and undogmatic.' *Scratch*

'An accomplished collection, well observed, powerful, controlled and thought-provoking.' *Ore*

'Acutely observed inner-city poems of place, which have simplicity and depth.' *Tears In The Fence*

£4.50

PRIVATE CITIES

with Joel Lane and Robin Lindsay Wilson

'In *Private Cities*, three writers share dreams, observations and experiences of urban living... Tony Lucas writing in measured tones, mostly from Brixton, is in the Eliot unreal city mould – yellow pools of lamplight, night and a steady sullen English rain sliding down the glass. Yet instead of lonely cab-horses steaming and stamping, we have cars and the noise of tyres on wet streets – and few poets write about them. Pale beams tunnel into night, reminscent of MacNeice's "The Wiper"... And in the manner of Betjeman's "Meditation on the A30" an executive seals up "the sixteen valve, two litre, fuel-injected privacies of his saloon". Stride's concept album is an appealing idea.' *Chapman*

'In Lucas' menacing world we are in his car or behind his curtains, alienated yet still unsafe, all focus channelled down into a seige mentality that we can feel eating away at the poet's consciousness. The best of these poems are understated and extremely harrowing. Excellent!' *Terrible Work*

£5.95

All books are available, post free, from the publisher:
STRIDE, 11 SYLVAN ROAD, EXETER, DEVON EX4 6EW
(cheques payable to 'Stride' please)